EFFECTIVE LIVING

Rayford Jones Elliott

This is a work of non-fiction. All scripture were taken from the King James Version and the English Standard Version of the Holy Bible, unless where otherwise noted.

CLF Publishing, LLC
www.clfpublishing.org
(909) 315-3161

Cover designed by Rayford J. Elliott.

ISBN# 978-1-945102-27-1

Printed in the United States of America.

Dedication

I dedicate this book to you, simply because you have this book in your hand and it is open. This implies to me that you have some interest in living an effective life; this type of life is where you put God at the head for your entire life. This warrants victory, success for you, along with a strong relationship with God.

As you read this book, feel the presence of God in all your surroundings. Don't just read this book, study it. Flood you heart with the Word of God. Your life will never be the same. God bless.

Acknowledgements

I want to acknowledge the Word of God which has been my foundation in living the type of life which God wants me to live. Through the wisdom I receive that builds and the understanding which establishes my life foundation, as I give myself to living and doing the work God has ordained me to do, I strive to be more effective in carrying out His will to the fullest of my ability. I give Him all the praises.

Table of Contents

Introduction

You will find on the following four pages a snapshot of the front and back pages of my Bible. My Bible had two blank pages, and I used them to record scripture that capture my heart spiritually.

As a believer who grew up in the church and broke away for years and finally returned, I have come to realize that while growing up I knew about Christ, but I didn't know Him.

As I began to sit and study the Word of God upon my return, as I listened to my pastor, read, study, attend Bible College, while being an active member of my church, I always found some scriptures that clung to my heart. I recorded them first on the back blank page of my Bible, and then finally, I used the front of my Bible as the list of scriptures increased. They have consistently been used as a reference, for meditation and study.

By doing so, I concluded that they assist me in living daily an effective life in the Word of God.

As the Bible is the infallible, unequivocal truth, it is the tool that every person should use to cling to an effective lifestyle as prescribed by it. It brings peace, love, and victory in every aspect of your life.

However, one must understand and know what is required of you from God. This is explained or pointed out in Deuteronomy 10:12-13, *"And now, Israel, what doth the LORD thy God require of thee, but to fear the LORD thy God, to walk in all his ways, and to love him, and to serve the LORD thy God with all thy heart and with all thy soul, To keep the commandments of the LORD, and his statutes, which I command thee this day for thy good?*

Also Micah 6:8 points out what is required also. *"He hath shewed thee, O man, what is good; and what doth the LORD require of thee, but to do justly, and to love mercy, and to walk humbly with thy God?"* Knowing what is required of you helps you to understand your purpose. By knowing your purpose, and if you so desire, you can live an effective life through the Word of God.

An effective life is not only a matter of being obedient, but to establish a true relationship with Jesus and the Father. Also an effective life will give you the strength, encouragement, and weapons you need to win any life battles as you live daily. These battles that you fight are physical, spiritual, social, and mental that manifest in your life daily. But we must remember that our battles are not just flesh and blood, but against principalities, powers, rulers of darkness of this world and spiritual wickedness in high places.

This book is divided in to three parts. Part I is "Effective Living Scripture," Part II is "Dealing with Challenges," and Part III is "The Effectivetudes."

There are four versions of the Bible that you will encounter throughout this book, The King James Version (KJV), The English Standard Version (ESV), the New Life Version (NLV) and the Holman Christian Standard Bible (HCSB).

In the scripture section, you will find the scripture quoted from the KJV and ESV. The second scripture is the same as the first but in a different version.

HOLY BIBLE

PRESENTED TO

Cyford Elliott

BY _____

_____

_____

_____

DATE _____

Scriptures on first page

PHILIPPIAN 3:13,14. BROTHERN I COUNT MYSELF TO
HAVE APPROHEN BUT THIS ONE THING I DO;
FORGETTING THOSE THINGS WHICH ARE BEHIND,
AND REACH FORTH UNTO THOSE THINGS WHICH ARE
BEFORE.
I PRESS TOWARD THE MARK FOR THE PRIZE
OF THE HIGH CALLING OF GOD IN CHRIST JESUS

PROVERB 20:24 Man's goings are of the Lord; how
can a Man then understand his own way

PROVERB 16:7 WHEN A MAN WAYS PLEASES THE
LORD, HE MAKE EVEN HIS ENEMIES TO BE AT
PEACE WITH HIM

PROVERB 3:5 Trust in the Lord with all thine
heart, and lean not unto thine own understanding

MATT 6:33,34 BUT SEEK YE FIRST THE KINGDOM OF GOD,
AND HIS RIGHTEOUSNESS; AND ALL THESE THINGS
SHALL BE ADDED UNTO YOU.
TAKE THEREFORE NO THOUGHT FOR THE MORROW:
FOR THE MORROW SHALL TAKE THOUGHT FOR THE
THINGS OF ITSELF, SUFFICIENT UNTO THE DAY
IS THE EVIL THEREOF.
JOHN 3:3 Except a man be born again
he cannot see the Kingdom of God
II CORN 12:9 My grace is sufficient for thee
for my strength is made perfect in weakness
most gladly therefore will I rather glory in
my infirmities that the power of Christ
may rest upon me

II CORINTHIAN 12:9,10 "MY GRACE IS SUFFICIENT FOR THEE:
FOR MY STRENGTH IS MADE PERFECT IN WEAKNESS."
MOST GLADLY THEREFORE WILL I RATHER GLORY IN MY
INFIRMITIES, THAT THE POWER OF CHRIST MAY REST
UPON ME.
10 THEREFORE I TAKE PLEASURE IN INFIRMITIES
IN REPROACHES, IN NECESSITIES, IN PERSECUTIONS,
IN DISTRESSES FOR CHRIST'S SAKE: FOR WHEN
I AM WEAK, THEN AM I STRONG.
EPH 2:4 BUT GOD WHO IS RICH IN MERCY, FOR HIS
LOVE WHEREWITH HE LOVED US,

WHAT WILL YOU DO IN INTEND TO PREPARE FOR
END TIME?

CHANGE IN MY LIFE

1. MY FINANCIAL SITUATION
2. MY RELATIONSHIP WITH MY PARTNER
3. MY SOUL WINNING
4. MY ABILITY TO DEAL & MAKE GOOD CHOICES
5. MY ABILITY TO LET THING GO WHEN NECESSARY
6. BETTER MANAGEMENT

II CORIN 4:8 WE ARE TROUBLED ON ALL SIDES

ECCLES ACTS 10:19 MONEY ANSWER COLL 3:17 DO IT IN NAME OF JESUS

I COR 10:13 ESCAPE TEMPTATION   GIVING - DEUT. 16:17

PROV 28:20 FAITFUL MAN BLESSING

MAT 12:31,32 - BLASPHEMY   CHRISTMAS SEEN I CORINTHIANS 8

PROV 23:7 AS HE THINKETH IN HIS HEART

2 SAM 4:18-19 DON'T HOLD ON TO YOUR PASS
PSALM 13:20 WHEN IN MIDST OF TROUBLE (RECIEVE HIM)   PAUL ADAPT TO SAVE I CORIN 9:15-23
II CORIN 4:8 S - HARD PRESS

PSALM 55:16 I WILL CALL UN TO THE LORD
ISAIAH 55:11 - MY WORD DO IT MY MOUTH
ISA - 41:2 - GOD BE WITH YOU
MALACHI 3:6 - GOD DON'T CHANGE
PSALM 91:1 - DWELL UNDER THE SHADOW OF THE ALMIGHTY
ACTS 1:8 - TO RECEIVE THE HOLY GHOST   CHRISTIAN TROUBLE PURPLE PERSECUTED

PSALM 66:2+3 CROOKED PLACE STRAIGHT
I JOHN 7 FELLOWSHIP

PROMISE OF HOLY SPIRIT   2 CORIN 4:8 5 PERPLEXED NOT dSPIR
I JOHN 10:16 - WILLFULL SIN
SCOUT YOURSELF WATCH PEE

JESUS TEACH LABOUR ARE FEW
29:11 I KNOW THE THOUGHT THAT I THINK
26:3 PERFECT PEACE   MICAH 6:8
18 DECREE A THING   DEUT 10

Scriptures from back page

SPEAKING IN TONGUE BENIFIT – 1 CORINTHIAN 14. 2,3,4
... GOT MARK 12:30,31   RINGING IN HEAD
COMMANDMENT   JER 29:01
THE   PSALM 50:14,15
GEN. 28:20-22 COMMUNE   LUKE 18:27
LEV. 27:30   1 CORN. 11:23 PSALM 37:5 COMMIT
                            HEB 10:23
15:16 – HE CHOOSE ME   PSALM 139:23-24 *

...ODHEAD – COLOSSIAN 2.9 – 10

HOW DO WE (GENTILE) RECEIVE PROMISE...
GALATIAN 3:14   PROPHECY
                                     JESUS IS COMING
CORN 9:18-23 ADAPT TO WHO YOU REACH ISAIAH 9:6
...13:23 ...   JOHN 10:9,10

MARK 1 "ALL'S POSSIBLE WITH GOD"   246 4 L
...ERAM. 1:5 "I ORDAINE YOU"
JOB 36:11 "SPEND UR DAYS IN PROSPERITY" V OBEY PROV 3:5...
                                     TITHE GEN 28:20
       33.3 I WILL ANSWER THEE & SHOW THEE
37:23 STEP OF A GOOD MAN   MAL. 3:8
    PS 139:23,24 – SEARCH & TRY ME 1 COR 9:6-8
                                JOB 22:28 DECREE THING
1:8-15 OBEY   PROV 3:1-6
AL 5:22 FRUIT OF SPIRIT   HEBREW 4:12-16
MENTATION 3.23 NOT CONSUMED   PETER 5:6-8
32:17 WORK OF RIGHTEOUSNESS   SCRIPTURE
                                 READING
ICH: 6.8 – WHAT GOD REQUIRE OF ME PSALM 113*
CORN 3:16 V TEMPLE OF GOD   PSALM 27
                                 1 JOHN 5:1-8
2:38 HOW TO RECEIVE THE HOLY SPIRIT PSALM 136
JERAMIAH 29 V PEACE   1 THESSALONIANS
...AH 43:2 PEACE IN THE STORM   4:13-17
TRANSFORMED 1 CORN 11:13, L4   PSALM 1:1-4
                                 PSALM 62:5-8
                                 1 CHRONICLES
                                 16:21-34
                                 PSALM 91:1-3
                                 DEUT. 28:1-8*

PART I

EFFECTIVE LIVING SCRIPTURES

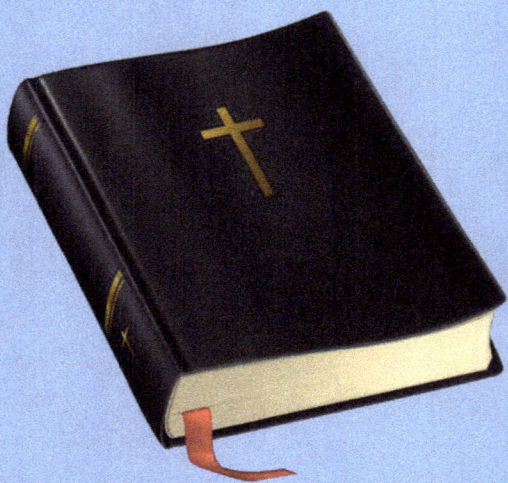

LOVE GOD

Mark 12:29-30

And Jesus answered him, The first of all the commandments is, Hear, O Israel; The Lord our God is one Lord: And thou shalt love the Lord thy God with all thy heart, and with all thy soul, and with all thy mind, and with all thy strength: this is the first commandment.

Jesus answered, "The most important is, 'Hear, O Israel: The Lord our God, the Lord is one. And you shall love the Lord your God with all your heart and with all your soul and with all your mind and with all your strength (ESV).

Loving God with all your heart means there is no glitch in the love affair. To love is to please, and it pleases God when He knows you truly love Him. Therefore, you will reap all the blessings He has for you. Loving God is effective living.

YOU ARE CHOSEN

John 15:16

Ye have not chosen me, but I have chosen you, and ordained you, that ye should go and bring forth fruit, and that your fruit should remain: that whatsoever ye shall ask of the Father in my name, he may give it to you.

You did not choose me, but I chose you and appointed you that you should go and bear fruit and that your fruit should abide, so that whatever you ask the Father in my name, he may give it to you (ESV).

As a believer, God chose you. That makes you special. Therefore, you are highly favored of God. As a chosen vessel, the blessings of God will flow through you daily. You will reap what you sow and produce fruit (bring others to get to know Him). As a producer and sower, you will develop the desire to touch others with what He has given you. Whenever you want something, ask Him, and it may be given to you according to His will. Asking God and producing fruit is effective living.

16

HE WANTS THE BEST FOR YOU

Jeremiah 29:11

For I know the thoughts that I think toward you, saith the LORD, thoughts of peace, and not of evil, to give you an expected end.

For I know the plans I have for you, declares the LORD, plans for welfare and not for evil, to give you a future and a hope (ESV).

Whatever you do in life, remember God has a plan for you, and He always wants the best for you. God's thoughts are His will; therefore, if He has thoughts of peace for you, you shall and will have peace in your life. Knowing God has a plan for your life is effective living.

TAKE YOU THROUGH

Psalm 50:14-15

Offer unto God thanksgiving; and pay thy vows unto
the most High: And call upon me in the day
of trouble: I will deliver thee, and thou shalt
glorify me.

Offer to God a sacrifice of thanksgiving, and perform
your vows to the Most High,
and call upon me in the day of trouble;
I will deliver you, and you
shall glorify me (ESV).

God will never abandon you in your time of trouble;
He will stick with you through all ordeals as He
extends His hand to you to pull you through. Knowing
God will pull you through your problems is effective
living.

GOD CAN MAKE THINGS HAPPEN

Luke 18:27

And he said, the things which are impossible with men are possible with God.

But he said, *"What is impossible with man is possible with God"* (ESV).

Even though things seem impossible to you at times, remember, God can make it happen if it is in His will for you. Relying on God to do the impossible for you is effective living.

COMMIT TO AND TRUST IN HIM

Psalm 37:5

Commit thy way unto the LORD; trust also in him; and he shall bring it to pass.

Commit thy way unto the LORD; trust also in him; and he shall bring it to pass (ESV).

Things may be tough on a daily basis, but if you commit and trust God, He will deliver you out of your troubles. He is aware of your struggles, and if you acknowledge Him, pray, and give thanks, you are living an effective life.

DON'T WAVER IN YOUR FAITH

Hebrews 10:23

Let us hold fast the profession of our faith without wavering; (for he is faithful that promised).

Let us hold fast the confession of our hope without wavering, for he who promised is faithful (ESV).

You cannot afford to go back and forth in your faith; temptation is constant. Therefore, you must be consistent in your belief and faith. Temptation is always knocking to try to get you to open the door to let it in. Consistency in faith is effective living.

YOU CAN BE CLEANSED

Psalm 139:23-24

Search me, O God, and know my heart: try me, and know my thoughts: And see if there be any wicked way in me, and lead me in the way everlasting.

Search me, O God, and know my heart! Try me and know my thoughts! And see if there be any grievous way in me, and lead me in the way everlasting (ESV)!

When you have sin problems you just cannot shake, allow God to search your heart and clean you. This process is done through forgiveness as the first step in allowing Him to cleanse you. All you need to do is ask, and He is faithful to forgive you. A clean heart makes way for effective living.

BUILD YOUR FAITH ON SOLID GROUND

Colossians 2:7-10

Rooted and built up in him, and stablished in the faith, as ye have been taught, abounding therein with thanksgiving. Beware lest any man spoil you through philosophy and vain deceit, after the tradition of men, after the rudiments of the world, and not after Christ.

Rooted and built up in him and established in the faith, just as you were taught, abounding in thanksgiving. See to it that no one takes you captive by philosophy and empty deceit, according to human tradition, according to the elemental spirits of the world, and not according to Christ (ESV).

Strong faith strengthens you. Strong faith will not allow you to become a captive to things of the world. Strong faith will help you become victorious. Strong faith is effective living.

23

BECOME ADAPTIVE

1 Corinthians 9:18-23

What is my reward then? Verily that, when I preach the gospel, I may make the gospel of Christ without charge, that I abuse not my power in the gospel. For though I be free from all men, yet have I made myself servant unto all, that I might gain the more. And unto the Jews I became as a Jew, that I might gain the Jews; to them that are under the law, as under the law, that I might gain them that are under the law; To them that are without law, as without law, (being not without law to God, but under the law to Christ,) that I might gain them that are without law. To the weak became I as weak, that I might gain the weak: I am made all things to all men, that I might by all means save some. And this I do for the gospel's sake, that I might be partaker thereof with you.

What then is my reward? That in my preaching I may present the gospel free of charge, so as not to make full use of my right in the Gospel. For though I am free from all, I have made myself a servant to all, that I might win more of them. To the Jews I became as a Jew, in order to win Jews. To those under the law I became as one under the law (though not being myself under the law) that I might win those under the law. To those outside the law I became as one outside the law (not being outside the law of God but under the law of Christ) that I might win those outside the law. To the weak I became weak, that I might win the weak. I have become all things to all people, that by all means I might save some. I do it all for the sake of the gospel, that I may share with them in its blessings (ESV).

It is advantageous to adapt to the situation you are dealing with though not become a part of it; you will better understand your foe. In your walk in life, you will meet all kinds and levels of people who communicate on different levels. Learning how to communicate with others according to their level is a gift from God. As you advance in the Word of God, this gift will manifest. Adapting to communicate is a spiritual ability and is effective living.

CONFESS YOUR FAITH

Hebrews 10:22-23

Let us draw near with a true heart in full assurance of faith, having our hearts sprinkled from an evil conscience, and our bodies washed with pure water. Let us hold fast the profession of our faith without wavering; (for he is faithful that promised)

Let us draw near with a true heart in full assurance of faith, with our hearts sprinkled clean from an evil conscience and our bodies washed with pure water. Let us hold fast the confession of our hope without wavering, for he who promised is faithful (ESV).

Listening, hearing, and saying the Word of God is communing with Him. Communion with God is effective living.

KNOW IT IS POSSIBLE

John 10:27

And Jesus looking upon them saith, With men it is impossible, but not with God: for with God all things are possible.

Jesus looked at them and said, "With man it is impossible, but not with God. For all things are possible with God" (ESV).

You may think there are some things in your life which seem impossible, but God can make them happen. The key is waiting on the Lord. You may be going through trials, or you may feel your life is broken, but be patient. God can fix it. Patience in life is effective living.

YOU ARE SANCTIFIED AND ORDAINED

Jeremiah 1:5

Before I formed thee in the belly I knew thee;
and before thou camest forth out of the womb
I sanctified thee, and I ordained thee a prophet
unto the nations.

*Before I formed you in the womb I knew you, and
before you were born I consecrated you; I appointed
you a prophet to the nations* (ESV).

God has sanctified and ordained you for the tasks you
will encounter in your life. God has a plan for you.
Recognizing and adhering to the appointed things God
has ordained you for is effective living.

LIVE IN OBEDIENCE AND PROSPERITY

Job 36:11

If they obey and serve him, they shall spend
their days in prosperity, and their years
in pleasures.

If they listen and serve him,
they complete their days in prosperity, and their years
in pleasantness (ESV).

There are great benefits in being obedient to the Word
of God; there is prosperity, love, joy, happiness,
strength, power, encouragement, endowment, peace,
and knowledge. Obedience is effective living.

LET HIM ANSWER AND SHOW YOU

Jeremiah 33:3

Call unto me, and I will answer thee, and show thee great and mighty things, which thou knowest not.

Call to me and I will answer you, and will tell you great and hidden things that you have not known (ESV).

When you call on God, wait for His answer. He will reveal to you all the things He wants for you; they are all good according to His Will. Pray that you will recognize God's answer. Recognizing God's answer is effective living.

KNOW WHAT YOUR ORDERS ARE

Psalm 37:23

The steps of a good man are ordered by the LORD: and he delighteth in his way.

The LORD shows us how we should live, and he is pleased when he sees people living that way (ESV).

The path you should follow and the way you should live is all in Scripture: His Word. Adhere to it, and it will lead you to live a victorious life, and there will be no condemnation. How you live can delight the Lord, if it is according to His righteousness. Delighting the Lord is effective living.

BE WILLING AND OBEY

Isaiah 1:18-19

Come now, and let us reason together, saith the LORD:
though your sins be as scarlet, they shall
be as white as snow; though they be red like crimson,
they shall be as wool. If ye be willing and obedient,
ye shall eat the good of the land:

*"Though your sins are like scarlet, they shall be
as white as snow; though they are red like crimson,
they shall become like wool. If you are willing and
obedient, you shall eat the good of the land"* (ESV).

Wash yourself from all evil things and present yourself
clean in the eyes of the Lord; your life will be
enlightened and you will live an effective life and enjoy
all of His benefits. Living a life of cleanliness from sin
is effective living.

ENJOY THE FRUIT OF THE SPIRIT

Galatians 5:22-23

But the fruit of the Spirit is love, joy, peace, longsuffering, gentleness, goodness, faith, meekness temperance.

But the fruit of the Spirit is love, joy, peace, patience, kindness, goodness, faithfulness, gentleness, self-control (ESV).

The fruit of the Spirit are products of spiritual growth, development, and maturity in the Word of God. These fruit are how Jesus Christ is manifested in you. These fruit are effective living.

DON'T ALLOW YOURSELF TO BE CONSUMED

Lamentations 3:22

It is of the LORD's mercies that we are not consumed, because his compassions fail not.

The steadfast love of the Lord never ceases; His mercies never come to an end (ESV).

The Lord's compassion for you is so great until His mercy is always working in your interest. The compassion of the Lord is manifested in His mercy, so that you may continue to walk in His spirit. His mercy is effective living.

THE EFFECT OF RIGHTEOUSNESS

Isaiah 32:17-18

And the work of righteousness shall be peace; and the effect of righteousness quietness and assurance forever. And my people shall dwell in a peaceable habitation, and in sure dwellings, and in quiet resting places.

And the effect of righteousness will be peace, and the result of righteousness, quietness and trust forever. My people will abide in a peaceful habitation, in secure dwellings, and in quiet resting places (ESV).

Righteous living brings peace, quietness, and assurance. Righteousness is effective living.

GOD WILL SUSTAIN YOU

Psalm 55:22

Cast thy burden upon the LORD, and he shall sustain thee: he shall never suffer the righteous to be moved.

Cast your burden on the Lord, and He will sustain you; he will never permit the righteous to be moved (ESV).

Be keep strong, steadfast, and encouraged as you pass through the river of trouble. Allow God to carry your burdens as you pass through. Handing your burdens over to Him is effective living.

VICTORY IN YOUR BATTLE

Psalm 55:18

He hath delivered my soul in peace from the battle that was against me: for there were many with me.

He redeems my soul in safety from the battle that I wage, for many are arrayed against me (ESV).

Let Him deliver you from evil and negative things in your life; He will bring you peace with your victory. There could be a thousand on your right hand and ten thousand on your side, and you may be alone, but He will deliver your victoriously from you battle. Deliverance from your enemy is effective living.

KNOW WHAT GOD REQUIRES OF YOU

Micah 6:8

He hath shewed thee O man, what is good; and what doth the LORD require of thee, but to do justly, and to love mercy, and to walk humbly with thy God?

He has told you, O man, what is good; and what does the LORD require of you but to do justice, and to love kindness, and to walk humbly with your God (ESV)?

Always meet your requirement and then add a little more. There are requirements God expects from you, and you must do them in order to please Him. When you do what is right according to His Word, love His mercy and walk humbly is effective living.

YOU ARE A LIVING TEMPLE

1 Corinthians 3:16

Know ye not that ye are the temple of God, and that the Spirit of God dwelleth in you? If any man defile the temple of God, him shall God destroy; for the temple of God is holy, which temple ye are.

Do you know that you are God's temple and that God's Spirit dwells in you? If anyone destroys God's temple, God will destroy him. For God's temple is holy, and you are that temple (ESV).

Protect your body, which is the temple of God, where the spirit dwells in you. Keep your faith strong and healthy. Your faith will help you keep your body in line with His Word. Allow your body to be the temple of God. The temple is holy and is a part of effective living.

HIS WORD WILL BURN IN YOU

Jeremiah 20:9

Then I said, I will not make mention of him, nor speak any more in his name. But his word was in mine heart as a burning fire shut up in my bones, and I was weary with forbearing, and I could not stay.

if I say," I will not mention him, or speak any more in his name," there is in my heart as it were a burning fire shut up in my bones, and I am weary with holding in, and I cannot (ESV).

Once His Word is embedded in your heart, you cannot help but to speak His word and praise Him. The Word of God that dwells inside you is effective living.

RECEIVE THE HOLY SPIRIT

Acts 2:38

Then Peter said unto them, Repent, and be baptized every one of you in the name of Jesus Christ for the remission of sins, and ye shall receive the gift of the Holy Ghost.

And Peter said to them, "Repent and be baptized every one of you in the name of Jesus Christ for the forgiveness of your sins, and you will receive the gift of the Holy Spirit (ESV).

After Peter and the other disciples were filled with the Holy Spirit at Pentecost, they took the gift of this experience to others. They received power when the Holy Spirit began to dwell in them. This power caused them to witness to others. They taught people to repent and be baptized. Via this power, people was healed, saved, and delivered. Open your heart to receive the Holy Spirit. The indwelling of the Holy Spirit is effective living.

PEACE UNTIL THE END

Jeremiah 29:11

For I know the thoughts that I think toward you, saith
the LORD, thoughts of peace, and not of evil,
to give you an expected end.

*For I know the plans I have for you, declares
the LORD, plans for welfare and not for evil, to give
you a future and a hope* (ESV).

As you continue to live in the Spirit, the plans God has
for you will manifest, and you will enjoy the life you
live with peace from the beginning to the end. God's
plan for you will always exist. He will keep you in
perfect peace if you keep your mind stayed on Him. To
live in perfect peace is effective living.

PROTECTED IN YOUR TRIBULATIONS

Isaiah 43:2

When thou passest through the waters, I will be with thee; and through the rivers, they shall not overflow thee: when thou walkest through the fire, thou shalt not be burned; neither shall the flame kindle upon thee.

When you pass through the waters, I will be with you; and through the rivers, they shall not overwhelm you; when you walk through fire you shall not be burned, and the flame shall not consume you (ESV).

In Him, wherever you go, He will protect you; do not fear your enemy. God is with you. Protection by God is effective living.

DISCERN DECEPTION

2 Corinthians 11:14-15

And no marvel; for Satan himself is transformed into an angel of light. Therefore it is no great thing if his ministers also be transformed as the ministers of righteousness; whose end shall be according to their works.

And no wonder, for even Satan disguises himself as an angel of light. So it is no surprise if his servant, also, disguise themselves as servant of righteousness. Their end will correspond to their deed (ESV).

Satan will allow his demons to preach the gospel: therefore, you must study the Word of God to show yourself approved. Once approved, you will have the ability to recognize deception from the enemy. Discernment of Satan's servants is effective living.

JESUS' COMING WAS PREDICTED

Isaiah 9:6

For unto us a child is born, unto us a son is given: and
the government shall be upon his shoulder: and his
name shall be called Wonderful, Counsellor, The
mighty God,
The everlasting Father,
the Prince of Peace.

*For to us a child is born, to us a son is given; and the
government shall be upon his shoulder, and his name
shall be called Wonderful Counselor, Mighty God,
Everlasting Father, Prince of Peace* (ESV).

It was known before Jesus came to earth that He was
coming to save us from our sin. Accepting Him as your
savior is effective living.

DONE BY THE SPIRIT

Zechariah 4:6

Then he answered and spake unto me, saying, This is
the word of the LORD unto Zerubbabel, saying, Not
by might, nor by power, but by my spirit, saith
the LORD of hosts.

*Then he said to me, "This is the word of the Lord to
Zerubbabel: Not by might, not by power, but by my
Spirit, says the Lord of Hosts* (ESV).

There is more power in the Spirit than in the physical
or natural. Thus, walk in the Spirit, and you will surely
have victory. The power of the Holy Spirit within you
will provide effective living.

DECREE A THING

Job 22:28

Thou shalt also decree a thing, and it shall be established unto thee: and the light shall shine upon thy ways.

You will decide on a matter, and it will be established for you, and light will shine on your ways (ESV).

Ask and you will receive, seek and you will find, knock and the door will open. Likewise, if you decree a thing, it will be established, and you will enjoy the fruit of the Spirit and have victory in life. When you decree a thing, it must come from your heart and out your mouth. To be established means it will be done. Jesus said in Mark 12:22-23: *"Have faith in God. Truly, I say to you, whoever says to this mountain, Be taken up and thrown into the sea, and does not doubt in his heart, but believes that what he says will come to pass, it will be done for him."* Decree it, but decree it in the name of Jesus. To decree a thing is effective living.

GOD SEES EVERYTHING

Hebrews 4:13

Neither is there any creature that is not manifest in his sight: but all things are naked and opened unto the eyes of him with whom we have to do.

And no creature is hidden from his sight, but all are neaked and exposed to the eyes of him to whom we must give account (ESV).

Whatever your do, even in the midst of your wrong doing or disobedience, God is always watching. Whatever is hidden; He sees it. He sees everything. Knowing God sees all is effective living.

HUMBLE YOURSELF

1 Peter 5:6-7

Humble yourselves therefore under the mighty hand of God, that he may exalt you in due time: Casting all your care upon him; for he careth for you.

Humble yourselves, therefore, under the mighty hand of God so that at the proper time he may exalt you, casting all your anxieties on him, because he cares for you (ESV).

You are not to submit yourself to man but unto God. When you submit to Him, you will be raised to a higher level in all aspects of your life. You will be highly favored. All of your trouble will be in His hand to lead you through. Submit to God, and He will take care of you and exalt you throughout your life. He does this because He loves you as a father loves His child. Casting all your cares on God is effective living.

STAND STRONG IN GOD'S WORD

1 Peter 5:8

Be sober, be vigilant; because your adversary the devil, as a roaring lion, walketh about, seeking whom he may devour:

Be sober-minded; be watchful. Your adversary the devil prowls around like a roaring lion, seeking someone to devour (ESV).

Your enemy always wants to defeat and destroy you. He wants to capture you and imprison you in his camp forever. But as you stand strong in God's Word, Satan will be defeated. Standing strong in your belief and faith is effective living.

DO IT IN JESUS' NAME

Colossians 3:17

And whatsoever ye do in word or deed, do all in the name of the Lord Jesus, giving thanks to God and the Father by him.

And whatever you do, in word or deed, do everything in the name of the Lord Jesus, giving thanks to God the Father through him (ESV).

It is imperative for you to understand God is involved either directly or indirectly in everything you do. Whatever your action is, let God know you are aware of His presence. Your actions, deeds, and words should be done with Jesus in mind; this can be done by giving thanks to God through Jesus by saying "in the name of Jesus." This is effective living.

PUT YOUR HEART IN IT

Colossians 3:16

Let the word of Christ dwell in you richly in all wisdom; teaching and admonishing one another in psalms and hymns and spiritual songs, singing with grace in your hearts to the Lord.

Let the word of Christ dwell in you richly, teaching and admonishing one another in all wisdom, singing psalms and hymns and spiritual songs, with thankfulness in your hearts to God (ESV).

Whenever you praise God, be it through song or prayer, by all means, make sure it comes from your heart, because the Word of Christ dwells in you. Praising from the heart is effective living.

YOU HAVE A WAY OUT

I Corinthians 10:13

There hath no temptation taken you but such as is common to man: but God is faithful, who will not suffer you to be tempted above that ye are able; but will with the temptation also make a way to escape, that ye may be able to bear it.

No temptation has overtaken you that is not common to man. God is faithful, and he will not let you be tempted beyond your ability, but with the temptation he will also provide the way of escape, that you may be able to endure it (ESV).

God always makes a way for you to not give into the temptation of sin. He keeps an open door to allow you to flee from sin and seek His blessings on the other side. Choosing the door God provides away from sin is effective living.

THE ONLY UNFORGIVEN SIN

Matthew 12:31-32

Wherefore I say unto you, All manner of sin and blasphemy shall be forgiven unto men: but the blasphemy against the Holy Ghost shall not be forgiven unto men.

Therefore I tell you, every sin and blasphemy will be forgiven people, but the blasphemy against the Spirit will not be forgiven (ESV).

There are literally hundreds of sins, and all can be forgiven with the exception of blasphemy of the Holy Spirit. God will not forgive this sin. Not blaspheming the Holy Spirit is effective living.

LET GO OF YOUR PAST

Isaiah 43:18-19

Remember ye not the former things, neither consider
the things of old. Behold, I will do a
new thing; now it shall spring forth; shall ye
not know it?

*Remember not the former things, nor consider the
things of old. Behold, I am doing a new thing;
now it springs forth, do you not
perceive it (ESV)?*

When your past becomes an impediment to your
present and future, let it go. God has better things for
you. Letting go of your past is effective living.

HE DELIVERS YOU FROM THE MIDST OF YOUR TROUBLE

Psalms 139:7

Though I walk in the midst of trouble, thou wilt revive me: thou shalt stretch forth thine hand against the wrath of mine enemies, and thy right hand shall save me.

Though I walk in the midst of trouble, you preserve my life; you stretch out your hand against the wrath of my enemies, and your right hand delivers me (ESV).

No matter what kind or how much trouble you are having, if you are abiding by His Word, He will bring you out favorably. Favor from God in times of trouble is effective living.

EXPERIENCE THE POWER OF GOD

2 Corinthians 4:8

We are troubled on every side, yet not distressed; we are perplexed, but not in despair: Persecuted, but not forsaken; cast down, but not destroyed.

We are afflicted in every way, but not crushed; perplexed, but not driven to despair; persecuted, but not forsaken; struck down, but not destroyed (ESV).

You are experiencing the power of God when you are not distressed, not in despair, not forsaken and not destroyed during the time of your troubles. Experiencing the power of God is effective living.

CALL HIM, HE SAVES

Psalm 55:16

As for me, I will call upon God; and the LORD
shall save me.

*But I call to God, and the LORD will
save me* (ESV).

Knock, and He will open the door. If you seek, then He
will allow you to find. If you ask, then He will answer
you. And if you call upon Him, He will save you. In
every trial, call upon the Lord. He will save you from
defeat and give you victory. He will save you from sin
and give you eternal life. Living a saved life is living
an effective life.

SPOKEN WORDS

Isaiah 55:11

So shall my word be that goeth forth out of my mouth: it shall not return unto me void, but it shall accomplish that which I please, and it shall prosper in the thing whereto I sent it.

So shall my word be that goes out from my mouth; it shall not return to me empty, but it shall accomplish that which I purpose, and shall succeed in the thing for which I sent it (ESV).

By studying, learning, and embedding the word within you, when you speak, your words will represent God's words. His spoken Word gives life. Living through His spoken Word is effective living.

PREACH CHRIST

2 Corinthians 4:5

For we preach not ourselves, but Christ Jesus the Lord; and ourselves your servants for Jesus' sake.

For what we proclaim is not ourselves, but Jesus Christ as Lord, with ourselves as your servants for Jesus' sake (ESV).

You must preach the Gospel and not exalt yourself. Preaching the Gospel of Jesus Christ makes the different between the lost and the saved, between right and wrong, between good and evil, between damnation and eternal life. Effective living is preaching the gospel of Christ.

GOD NEVER CHANGES

Malachi 3:6

For I am the LORD, I change not; therefore ye
sons of Jacob are not consumed.

For I the Lord do not change; therefore you, O
children of Jacob, are not consumed (ESV).

God is the same yesterday, today, and forever.
Therefore, what He promises will endure. And His
promises can keep you from becoming consumed by
your enemy as long as you exist on this earth. Knowing
God's promises is effective living.

HIS SHADOW IS PROTECTION

Psalm 91:1

He that dwelleth in the secret place of the most High shall abide under the shadow of the Almighty.

He who dwells in the shelter of the Most High will abide in the shadow of the Almighty (ESV).

If your shadow is attacked, no harm can be done to it not matter what is done. When you stand in God's shadow, no matter what the enemy tries to do to you, it will be to no avail. Therefore, the enemy cannot touch you in any way or form. God's shadow is protection. Living in God's shadow is effective living.

A PRAYER

Heavenly Father,

We come to you today with open ears, mind, and heart to hear what you have to say. If there has been any drifting away for your word, we ask you to restore us to the joy of your salvation. Anytime a hardened heart tries to creep into us, restore us to meekness and humbleness. Anytime sadness creeps in, settle us. Anytime doubt creeps in us, restore us to the unity of our faith. Anytime wavering comes in us, restore us to keep our mind stayed on you.

Amen.

LET HIM DO IT, FOR HE IS GOD

Isaiah 45:2-3

I will go before thee, and make the crooked places straight: I will break in pieces the gates of brass, and cut in sunder the bars of iron: And I will give thee the treasures of darkness, and hidden riches of secret places, that thou mayest know that I, the LORD, which call thee by thy name, am the God of Israel.

"I *will go before you and level the exalted places, I will break in pieces the doors of bronze and cut through the bars of iron, I will give you the treasures of darkness and the hoards in secret places, that you may know that it is I, the Lord, the God of Israel, who call you by your name"* (ESV).

Our God is the God Almighty, the one and only God, the great I AM, and He can do all things. He will straighten out your path, so you can see where you are going. He will make sure all of your needs are met with surplus, so you can delight in him. Give all of your burdens to Him. He will make things right for you. There is nothing too hard for God to do. Believing God will make a way for you is effective living.

BE AWARE OF "APOSTLES"

2 Corinthians 11:13-14

For such are false apostles, deceitful workers, transforming themselves into the apostles of Christ. And no marvel; for Satan himself is transformed into an angel of light.

For such men are false apostles, deceitful workmen, disguising themselves as apostles of Christ. And no wonder for even Satan disguises himself as an angel of light (ESV).

It is advantageous to understand that Jesus Christ made or appointed apostles. You can see this in Bible history. True apostles are not appointed by man. Trust in God not man. That is effective living.

THE WONDERFUL ONE

Isaiah 9:6

For unto us a child is born, unto us a son is given: and the government shall be upon his shoulder: and his name shall be called Wonderful, Counsellor, The mighty God, The everlasting Father, the Prince of Peace.

For to us a child is born, to us a son is given; and the government shall be upon his shoulder, and his name shall be called Wonderful Counselor, Mighty God, Everlasting Father, Prince of Peace (ESV).

The Wonderful one who is known as Jesus Christ is the Son of God. He is the prince of peace. He came to give peace in life and everlasting life to all who want it. Recognizing Jesus is the Son of God is effective living.

YOU CAN BE SAVED

John 10:9-10

ɪ am the door: by me if any man enter in, he shall be
saved, and shall go in and out, and find pasture. The
thief cometh not, but for to steal, and to kill, and to
destroy: I am come that they might have life, and that
they might have it more abundantly.

I am the door. If anyone enters by me, he will be
saved and will go in and out and find pasture. The
thief comes only to steal and kill and destroy. I came
that they may have life and have it
abundantly (ESV).

The door to salvation is open with Jesus standing at the
open door asking you to come in. This door is for
anyone who wants to have peace on earth and eternal
life in heaven. The enemy is always working to destroy
you, to make you unfit for the blessings of God. But
Jesus opens the door for you to live an abundant life.
An abundant life is effective living.

TRUST FROM YOUR HEART

Proverbs 3:5

Trust in the Lord with all thine heart; and lean not
unto thine own understanding.

*Trust in the LORD with all your heart, and do not lean
on your own understanding* (ESV).

Your understanding does not always reflect the truth.
It can be wrong. Therefore, it is wise to let your heart
be your guide. Your heart is where the Word of God is
hidden. Psalm 119:11 says, *"Thy Word have I hid in
mine heart, that I might not sin against thee."* With the
Word in your heart, your trust is genuine. Hiding God's
Word in your heart is effective living.

HE KEEPS, FEEDS AND PROTECTS

Genesis 28:20

And Jacob vowed a vow, saying, If God will be with me, and will keep me in this way that I go, and will give me bread to eat, and raiment to put on.

Then Jacob made a vow, saying, "If God will be with me and will keep me in this way that I go, and will give me bread to eat and clothing to wear (ESV).

By honoring, praising, worshiping and glorifying Him, He will always make provisions and protect you from the enemies when you are having a tempestuous experience in life. You don't have to worry about tomorrow or the present, God will provide and protect you. Relying on Him to provide and protect you is effective living.

KEEP KINDNESS AND TRUTH IN YOUR LIFE

Proverb 3:1-8

My son, do not forget my teaching. Let your heart keep my words. For they will add to you many days and years of life and peace. Do not let kindness and truth leave you. Tie them around your neck. Write them upon your heart. So you will find favor and good understanding in the eyes of God and man. Trust in the Lord with all your heart, and do not trust in your own understanding. Agree with Him in all your ways, and He will make your paths straight. Do not be wise in your own eyes. Fear the Lord and turn away from what is sinful. It will be healing to your body and medicine to your bones.

Being kind and truthful is effective living.

GOD'S WORD DISCERNS THE HEART AND THOUGHTS

Hebrews 4:12

For the word of God is quick, and powerful, and sharper than any two edged sword, piercing even to the dividing asunder of soul and spirit, and of the joints and marrow, and is a discerner of the thoughts and intents of the heart.

For the word of God is living and active, sharper than any two-edge sword, piercing to the division of soul and of soul and of spirit, of joints and of marrow, and discerning the thoughts and intentions of the heart (ESV).

When you let the Word of God guide you, mold you, build you and be the keeper of your heart, it is more powerful and sharper than any two-edged sword. Letting God discern the thoughts and intentions of your heart is effective living.

GOD EYES ARE UPON YOU

Deuteronomy 11:12-13

A land which the Lord thy God careth for: the eyes of the LORD thy God are always upon it, from the beginning of the year even unto the end of the year.

A land that the LORD your God cares for. The eyes of the LORD your God are always upon it, from the beginning of the year to the end of the year (ESV).

As He takes care of His land, He will take care of you. When you give your life to serving God, He will bless your abundantly. He will watch over you day and night, from the beginning to the end of time. Knowing God cares and watches over you is effective living.

HARKEN UNTO HIS VOICE

Deuteronomy 28:1-2

And it shall come to pass, if thou shalt hearken diligently unto the voice of the LORD thy God, to observe and to do all his commandments which I command thee this day, that the LORD thy God will set thee on high above all nations of the earth: And all these blessings shall come on thee, and overtake thee, if thou shalt hearken unto the voice of the LORD thy God.

And if you faithfully obey the voice of the LORD your God, being careful to do all his commandments that I command all the nations of the earth. And all these blessings shall come upon you and overtake you, if you obey the voice of the LORD your God (ESV).

If one is looking for many rewards in life, there are many to be received. The blessings mentioned here are your reward from God. They are unlimited. However, they are not without stipulations: You must be obedient to His Word. If so, He will set you upon high grounds. The enemy will not be able to touch you with his destructive weapons to prevent you from receiving. You will enjoy all the fruit and benefits God has for you all the days of your life. God's overtaking blessings, through His grace, is effective living.

PAY AND CALL

Psalm 15: 14-15

Offer unto God thanksgiving; and pay thy vows unto the most High: And call upon me in the day of trouble: I will deliver thee, and thou shalt glorify me.

Offer to God a sacrifice of thanksgiving, and perform your vows to the Most High, and call upon me in the day of trouble; I will deliver you, and you shall glorify me (ESV).

You must recognize everything God does for you. He is always providing for you and making a way. He will keep you on high ground, so the enemy cannot defeat you. Vow to Him, give Him thanks, and continue to call on Him in times of need. Calling on Him in times of need is effective living.

IT IS POSSIBLE

Luke 18:27

And he said, The things which are impossible with men are possible with God.

But he said, "What is impossible with man is possible with God" (ESV).

As you advance in life, you will run into obstacles. Some will be tantamount, and it may appear that there is no way you can overcome them. But remember to rely on God. And if it is His will, you can overcome any obstacle that gets in your way with victory via God's power. Overcoming obstacles through God is effective living.

BRING IT TO PASS

Psalm 37:5

Commit thy way unto the LORD; trust also in him; and
he shall bring it to pass.

*Commit your way to the LORD; trust in him, and he
will act* (ESV).

There are 518 mentions of the phrase "shall pass" in
the KJV Bible. This indicates all we are going through
sooner or later will end. However, trusting in God as
you go through will be favorable to you in the end. He
will be with you every step of the way and give you
guidance and encouragement as you move along.
Commit your ways to God and delight yourself in Him.
He will give you the desires of your heart and assist
you in overcoming your problems favorably in Jesus'
name. That is effective living.

STAY STEADY IN YOU FAITH

Hebrews 10:23

Let us hold fast the profession of our faith without wavering; (for he is faithful that promised)

Let us hold fast the confession of our hope without wavering, for he who promised is faithful (ESV).

The one who died for us still lives with us. His presence helps strengthen us. Via direct access, today His presence is with you. Therefore, don't waver in your faith in Him, because your faith will please Him to do for you. Effective living is not wavering in your faith.

A PRAYER

We give ourselves to you oh mighty God. Take our hand oh Lord and lead us to the path of righteousness oh God. Take our hand and lead us to the path of knowledge of you. Take our hand and lead us to the path of love. Take our hand and lead us to the path of meekness. Take our hand oh Lord and lead us to humbleness, take our hand oh Lord and lead us to healing, Take our hand oh Lord and lead us to the path of peace. Take our hand and lead us to the path of forgiveness oh Lord. Lead us oh Lord as we give ourselves away to You.

FIX ME FOR EVERLASTING

Psalm 139:23-24

Search me, O God, and know my heart: try me,
and know my thoughts: And see if there be any
wicked way bin me, and lead me in
the way everlasting.

*Search me, O God, and know my heart! Try me and
know my thoughts! And see if there be any grievous
way in me, and lead me in the way
everlasting (ESV)!*

Like so many things, sometimes our spiritual and
natural lives need to have a diagnosis run on them. We
must do so to see if there are any weaknesses or any
flaws we may have overlooked, so there are no
openings in our life that Satan could attack to try and
penetrate our life with his evil ways. That is why we
need to allow God to run the test on us, so we can find
the area we need strength. We want to do what is right,
so we will have everlasting life with Him. Everlasting
is effective living.

HOW TO BRING IT TO PASS

Psalm 37:5

Commit thy way unto the Lord; trust also in him; and he shall bring it to pass.

Commit your way to the LORD; trust in him, and he will act (ESV).

There are so many times when things happen and seem to linger on in life. The struggle is tense and difficult. Sometimes, there is no visible way out. We are pressing toward the mark, but there seems to be no end; however, if you would commit to the Lord, He will bring you out. He will not only bring you out, He will give you peace as you go through it. Your commitment and His peace will bring you to victory. Committing is effective living.

GROW INTO HIS IMAGE

Ephesians 4:15

But speaking the truth in love, may grow up into him in all things, which is the head, even Christ:

Rather, speaking the truth in love, we are to grow up in every way into Him who is the head, into Christ (ESV).

We are to be like Christ. That is, taking on His characteristics. Some of His characteristics are love, joy, peace, happiness, longsuffering, faith, humbleness, and meekness. Efforts should be made throughout our life to be like Christ. Scripture also tells us we should take on His image and display it wherever we go in life: to the supermarket, job, vacations, etc, not just in church. Being the image of Christ is effective living.

THE LIFE GOD WANTS FOR YOU

John 10:10

The thief cometh not, but for to steal, and to kill, and
to destroy: I am come that they might have life, and
that they might have it more abundantly.

The thief comes only to steal and kill and destroy.
I came that they may have life and have it abundantly
(ESV).

It is clear what Satan's purpose is. He is evil and
destructive. He wants every man to fall into his
dominion. There is no righteousness or good on his
agenda. But Jesus is full of love, and He desires for you
to have an abundant life, full of riches in love,
happiness, and finances. Abundance in these things
and the life God has prepared for you is effective
living.

MAKE YOUR CHOICE

Deuteronomy 30:19

I call heaven and earth to record this day against you,
that I have set before you life and death, blessing and
cursing: therefore choose life, that
both thou and thy seed may live.

*I call heaven and earth to witness against you today,
that I have set before you life and death, blessing,
curse. Therefore choose life, that you and your
offspring may live* (ESV).

God wants you to make the correct choices in life
because the choices will not just affect you now and
your offspring but in the future as well. Therefore, the
correct choice is God. With God, there is everlasting
life. Choosing everlasting life with God is effective
living.

GOD HAS PREPARED

1 Corinthians 2:9

But as it is written, Eye hath not seen, nor ear heard, neither have entered into the heart of man, the things which God hath prepared for them that love him.

But, as it is written, "What no eye has seen, nor ear heard, nor the heart of man imagined, what God Has prepared for those who love Him" (ESV).

As you look back, you can see many blessings you have received. Thus, your future is secure in Jesus Christ. He has prepared eternal life for you with love, everlasting peace, happiness, no sorrow, and no troubles that will never depart from you. Knowing this should encourage you to live the life God has prescribed for you to live here on earth: a life to render service to Him and worship Him. By doing this, you will live your life to the fullest and enjoy all of its benefits. Recognizing the prepared life God has set in place for you is effective living.

THE SPIRIT FLOWS
IN YOU

Proverb 4:23

Keep thy heart with all diligence; for out of it are the issues of life.

Keep your heart with all vigilance,
for from it flow the springs of life (ESV).

Your spiritual life flows from the heart. The Word of God reveals to you the thoughts and intents of the heart. Therefore, make sure the Word of God is in your heart because the heart can become infected via spiritual warfare with the enemy which you encounter every day. Let the Word of God flow through you like running water. The Word of God flows in you, waters the Spirit in you, and causes you to be stronger in life. The Word of God flowing in you is effective living.

THINGS WORK FOR THE GOOD IN YOUR LIFE

Roman 8:28

And we know that for those who love God all things work together for good, for those who are called according to his purpose.

We know that God makes all things work together for the good of those who love Him and are chosen to be a part of His plan (ESV).

God is good! Therefore, there is nothing but goodness flowing from Him. Always position yourself for the working of good things to flow in your life. This will keep everything working for your good. It may not be perfect, but it will pave a way for your needs and desires to be met. A life working for your good is effective living.

COMFORT OTHERS

2 Corinthians 1:3-4

Blessed be God, even the Father of our Lord Jesus Christ, the Father of mercies, and the God of all comfort; Who comforteth us in all our tribulation, that we may be able to comfort them which are in any trouble, by the comfort wherewith we ourselves are comforted of God.

Blessed be the God and Father of our Lord Jesus Christ, the Father of mercies and God of all comfort, who comforts us in all our affliction, so that we may be able to comfort those who are in any affliction, with the comfort with which we ourselves are comforted by God (ESV).

Effective living is through the comfort God provides you. As you are comforted by Him, you are to work toward making others comfortable in the name of Jesus.

REACH FOR WHAT IS AHEAD

Philippians 3:13

Brethren, I count not myself to have apprehended: but this one thing I do, forgetting those things which are behind, and reaching forth unto those things which are before.

Brothers, I do not consider that I have made it my own. But one thing I do: forgetting what lies behind and straining forward to what lies ahead (ESV).

Looking back while you are running a race while the finish line is ahead can cause you to not reach the mark on the finish line. One often looks back at defeats and failures in his/her life; the effect is it can cause you to miss the finish line of your present race. You will miss the mark. Focus on what God has assigned to you, and you will surely win. It is effective living to focus and keep your mind stayed on Jesus as you move forward in life.

LET YOUR STEPS BE GUIDED

Proverbs 20:24

Man's goings are of the LORD; how can a man then understand his own way?

A man's steps are from the LORD; how then can man understand his way (ESV)?

No man has absolute control of his life. As you live, there is an element of control from some other entities. Sometime the entity can assume control. Thus, your life could be heading to destruction or damnation via the wrong leader, namely Satan. On the other hand, your life can be led to prosperity, abundant living full of love and caring, open doors of opportunity here on earth, and everlasting life in heaven- if you would allow God to guide your steps daily. God guiding your steps in life is effective living.

YOUR ENEMIES AT PEACE WITH YOU

Proverbs 16:7

When a man's ways please the LORD, he maketh even his enemies to be at peace with him.

When the ways of a man are pleasing to the Lord, He makes even those who hate him to be at peace with him (NLV).

When the heart is deceitful and wicked, God is not pleased. With a righteous heart, worship, and praises, the Lord is pleased. As you please God, the enemy will attack and try to sway you over to his ways. God recognizes your struggle, and He will make your enemies be at peace with you. That gives you the advantage. God's advantage in your life is effective living.

ESTABLISH A RELATIONSHIP

John 3:3

Jesus answered and said unto him, Verily, verily, I say unto thee, Except a man be born again, he cannot see the kingdom of God.

Jesus said to him, "For sure, I tell you, unless a man is born again, he cannot see the holy nation of God" (ESV).

The lawyer Nicodemus wanted to know from Jesus "How can a man be born again?" What it means when Jesus made the statement that you must be "born again" is He wants more than just obedience to the commandments. There must be a relationship with the Father. A fervent, strong relationship established with God, abiding by His Word is effective living. A relationship with God is effective living.

THE POWER OF CHRIST IN YOU

2 Corinthians 12:9-10

And he said unto me, My grace is sufficient for thee; for my strength is made perfect in weakness. Most gladly therefore will I rather glory in my infirmities, that the power of Christ may rest upon me. Therefore I take pleasure in infirmities, in reproaches, in necessities, in persecutions, in distresses for Christ's sake: for when I am weak, then am I strong.

But he said to me, "My grace is sufficient for you, for my power is made perfect in weakness." Therefore I will boast all the more gladly of my weaknesses, so that the power of Christ may rest upon me. For the sake of Christ, then, I am content with weaknesses, insults, hardships, persecutions, and calamities. For when I am weak, then I am strong (ESV).

As you go through life, you will find yourself sometimes weak in your struggles. There will be times you will have hardships, and there will be times you are persecuted by your enemy. But these are times that you are tested and find yourself molded to withstand the attacks. You will grow stronger. This is a great opportunity to fortify your faith in God. The power of Christ rests upon and with you as you go through. The power of Christ in you is effective living.

FIRST THING YOU MUST DO

Matthew 6:33

But seek ye first the kingdom of God, and his righteousness, and all these things will be added to you.

But seek first the kingdom of God and his righteousness, and all these things will be added to you (ESV).

There are so many things available for you in this life. We all have desires and needs. But to receive the fullest of things that are stored for you in the form of blessings, you must seek to be a part of God's Kingdom. Thus, you don't have to worry about what you eat, what you wear, or what you drink. Your heavenly Father knows all your needs and will surely supply them to you. Keep Him in the forefront of your life. As a part of His kingdom, God's blessings will rain down on you. Seeking His kingdom is effective living.

DON'T WORRY ABOUT TOMORROW

Matthew 6:34

Take therefore no thought for the morrow: for the morrow shall take thought for the things of itself. Sufficient unto the day is the evil thereof.

Therefore do not be anxious about tomorrow, for tomorrow will be anxious for itself. Sufficient for the day is its own trouble (ESV).

We all plan for the future. This is something Jesus wants us to do. Plan, but do not worry about it. Know that it's all in God's hand. We should focus on the present and make sure our plan for eternal life with God is set forth. Not worrying is effective living.

KEEP AWAY FROM MISCHIEF

Proverbs 24:1-3

Be not thou envious against evil men, neither desire to be with them. For their heart studieth destruction, and their lips talk of mischief. Though wisdom is an house builded; and by understanding it is established.

Be not envious of evil men, nor desire to be with them, for their hearts devise violence, and their lips talk of trouble. By wisdom a house is built, and by understanding it is established (ESV).

Wisdom, understanding, and knowledge are keys to building a house, likewise in building your spiritual life. Having wisdom, understanding, and know-ledge are effective living.

ALL THINGS ARE POSSIBLE

Mark 10:27

And Jesus looking upon them saith, With men it is impossible, but not with God; for with God all things are possible.

Jesus looked at them and said, "With man it is impossible, but not with God. For all things are possible with God" (ESV).

God is a sovereign god, which means He is the creator and all power is in His hand. Whatever His will is, it shall be. You may find yourself in seemly impossible situations, but remember with God, it can be possible. On the other hand, you must remember also if it is all in the confinement of God's will, learn to accept His will. God doing the impossible for you is effective living.

YOU HAVE THE POWER

Luke 10:19

Behold, I give unto you power to tread on serpents
and scorpions, and over all the power of the enemy;
and nothing shall by any means hurt you.

*Behold, l have given you authority to tread on
serpents and scorpions, and over all the power of the
enemy, and nothing shall hurt you* (ESV).

The serpents and scorpions symbolize Satan who is the
enemy, who always wants to harm you by getting you
to yield to his ways. Jesus has given you the power to
say no to evil. It is simple. Recognize and use your
God-given power. Your God-given power being used
is effective living.

PROMOTION IN LIFE

Psalm 75:6-7

For promotion cometh neither from the east, nor from the west, nor from the south. But God is the judge: he puteth down one, and setteth up another.

For not from the east or from the west and not from the wilderness come lifting up, but it is God who executes judgment, putting down one and lifting up another (ESV).

There is always promotion in life that awaits you. God is by far the best promoter. If you are with Him, He will promote or elevate you in every aspect of your life. Get with God and stay with Him. There are great benefits you know not of. Promotion and elevation in life is effective living.

SEVEN BENEFITS TO KNOWING HIM

Psalm 91:14-16

Because he hath set his love upon me, therefore will I deliver him: I will set him on high. Because he hath known my name. He shall call upon me, and I will answer him: I will be with him in trouble; I will deliver him, and honor him. With long life I will satisfy him, and shew him my salvation.

Because he holds fast to me in love, I will deliver him; I will protect him, because he knows my name. When he calls to me, I will answer him; I will be with him in trouble; I will rescue him and honor him. With long life I will satisfy him and show him my salvation
(ESV).

If you would only get to know Him, praise Him, worship Him, love Him, honor Him and glorify Him, then you would be in line for seven key benefits. During your stay here on earth, you will receive deliverance, protection, answers to your prayers, support in times of trouble, long life, salvation, and love. Having deliverance, protection, answers to prayers, support, long life, salvation and love is effective living.

YOUR REFUGE

Psalm 91:1-2

He that dwelleth in the secret place of the most High shall abide under the shadow of the Almighty. I will say of the Lord, He is my refuge and my fortress: my God; in him I trust.

He who dwells in the shelter of the Most High will abide in the shadow of the Almighty. I will say to the LORD, "My refuge and my fortress, my God, in whom I trust" (ESV).

When you walk, talk, and live in the mighty Word of God, He will make sure there will be a refuge for you if needed - in Him. When times of adversities, stress, despair and needs, He will be the hand that will pull you through and in the process keep you encouraged and uplifted at all times. In this state, you are better able to deal with your trials and tribulations. He will place you where all of your enemies will not be able to touch or affect you. Though you are attacked from all directions, His refuge will keep you safe. Take refuge in the Lord; that is effective living.

HE LIGHTS YOUR PATH

Psalm 119:105

Thy word is a lamp unto my feet, and a light unto my path.

Your word is a lamp to my feet and a light to my path (ESV).

Open your spiritual and physical eyes, so you can see the pathway you are traveling through in life. Through God, your path is visible through the spiritual lamp the Lord has placed at your feet so you will not stumble. He has placed a light in your pathway, so you can see your destination at the end of tunnel. Jesus, who is your destination, is where He wants you to go. The light you strive for is effective living.

THINGS HAPPEN TO YOU IN SEASONS

Ecclesiastes 3:1

To everything there is a season, and a time to every purpose under the heaven:

For everything there is a season, and a time for every matter under heaven (ESV).

God does all things for us according to His will and His time. Therefore, there is no place for us in life to be impatient. Patience is effective living.

KEEP YOUR CONFIDENCE

1 John 5:14

And this is the confidence that we have in him, that, if we ask any thing according to his will, he heareth us.

And this is the confidence that we have toward him, that if we ask anything according to his will he hears us (ESV).

Confidence is a manifestation of faith. With faith, through Jesus Christ, you can do all things according to His will. When you ask for something, believe through your faith that God will hear you as you ask. But remember God's will is greater than your will. The confidence you have through faith is effective living.

PETITION FOR WHAT YOU WANT

1 John 5:15

And if we know that he hear us, whatsoever we ask, we know that we have the petitions that we desired of him.

And if we know that he hears us in whatever we ask, we know that we have the requests that we have asked of him (ESV).

To petition is to request. We practically petition every day in our life. A lot of the time, it is to no avail. When we petition to God, we know without a doubt He hears us. Our desires will be met according to His will. Petitioning God is effective living.

A MATTER OF ASKING

John 11:22

But I know, that even now, whatsoever thou wilt ask
of God, God will give it thee.

*"But even now I know that whatever you ask from
God, God will give you"* (ESV).

Luke 18:27 says, *"What is impossible with man is
possible with God; since this is the case then all you
have to do is ask Him."* Sometimes, you don't see your
way out, but remember, God is sovereign. All power is
in His hands, and there is nothing He cannot do. If you
want victory, He will provide success. If you want
healing, He will heal. If you want encouragement, He
will provide. If you need help, He will provide it. If you
need vision, He will provide it. If you need deliverance,
He will provide it. If you need direction, He will
provide it. All these things come according to His will
by just asking. Asking God is effective living.

WHAT TO FOLLOW AFTER

1 Timothy 6:11

But thou, O man of God, flee these things; and follow after righteousness, godliness, faith, love, patience, meekness.

But as for you, O man of God, flee these things. Pursue righteousness, godliness, faith, love, steadfastness, gentleness (ESV).

Watch what you pursue. One's passion is usually displayed in what he/she pursues. Pursue evil, and you will get evil. Pursue righteousness, and you get righteousness. Watch your motives, your testimony, and your values. Be aware of signs and wonders. Pursuing things that are of the will of God is effective living.

SAVE YOURSELF

Ephesians 3:8-9

For by grace are ye saved through faith; and that not of yourselves: it is the gift of God: Not of works, lest any man should boast.

For by grace you have been saved through faith. And this is not your own doing; it is the gift of God, not a result of works, so that no one may boast (ESV).

Jesus Christ came and made it possible for us to be saved, to be saved from our enemy's weapon: sin. Jesus saves, but it is predicated on the grace of God and your faith. This is not of yourself but your stand with Jesus. Living a saved life through faith is effective living.

KNOW THAT THERE ARE BENEFITS

Psalm 103:2

Bless the Lord, O my soul,
and forget not all his benefits.

*My soul, praise the Lord,
and do not forget all His benefits* (HCSB).

To bless the Lord is to praise Him. Benefits mean paying back what is deserved. You receive benefits from the Lord because of your praises. He wants you to praise Him, and that opens the door for you to receive from Him all He desires for you. Receiving God's benefits is effective living.

LIVE FOREVER

Isaiah 40:8

The grass withereth, the flower fadeth: but the word
of our God shall stand for ever.

*The grass withers, the flowers fade,
but the word of our God remains forever* (HCSB).

Ordinarily, people have short life. That is, their life is
the extent of the time they are on earth. But on the other
hand, all can have an everlasting life. This is achieved
through the Word of God. Heaven and earth will fade
away, but the Word of God will live forever. Therefore,
allowing the Word of God to live in you will create an
everlasting life. An everlasting life is effective living.

PART II

DEALING WITH CHALLENGES

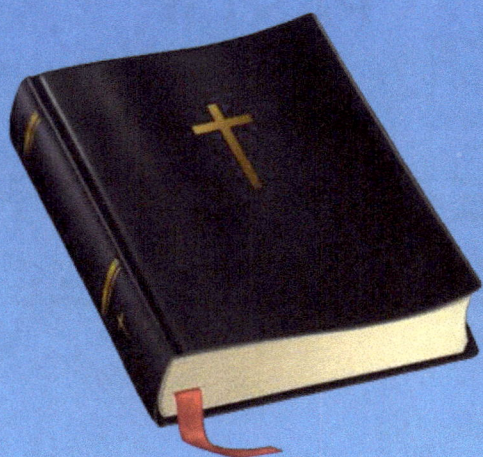

WHEN YOUR FAITH NEEDS STIRRING

"Now faith is the substance of things hoped for, the evidence of things not seen. For by it the elders obtained a good report. Through faith we under-stand that the worlds were framed by the word of God, so that things which are seen were not made of things which do appear.

By faith Abel offered unto God a more excellent sacrifice than Cain, by which he obtained witness that he was righteous, God testifying of his gifts: and by it he being dead yet speaketh.

By faith Enoch was translated that he should not see death; and was not found, because God had translated him: for before his translation he had this testimony, that he pleased God. But without faith it is impossible to please him: for he that cometh to God must believe that he is, and that he is a rewarder of them that diligently seek him.

By faith Noah, being warned of God of things not seen as yet, moved with fear, prepared an ark to the saving of his house; by the which he condemned the world, and became heir of the righteousness which is by faith.

By faith Abraham, when he was called to go out into a place which he should after receive for an inheritance, obeyed; and he went out, not knowing whither he went.

By faith he sojourned in the land of promise, as in a strange country, dwelling in tabernacles with Isaac and Jacob, the heirs with him of the same promise: For he looked for a city which hath foundations, whose builder and maker is God.

By faith Abraham, when he was tried, offered up Isaac: and he that had received the promises offered up his only begotten son, Of whom it was said, That in Isaac shall thy seed be called: Accounting that God was able to raise him up, even from the dead; from whence also he received him in a figure.

By faith Isaac blessed Jacob and Esau concerning things to come. By faith Jacob, when he was a dying, blessed both the sons of Joseph; and worshipped, leaning upon the top of his staff. By faith Joseph, when he died, made mention of the departing of the children of Israel; and gave commandment concerning his bones.

By faith Moses, when he was born, was hid three months of his parents, because they saw he was a proper child; and they were not afraid of the king's commandment.

By faith Moses, when he was come to years, refused to be called the son of Pharaoh's daughter; Choosing rather to suffer affliction with the people of God, than to enjoy the pleasures of sin for a season; Esteeming the reproach of Christ greater riches than the treasures in Egypt: for he had respect unto the recompence of the reward.

By faith he forsook Egypt, not fearing the wrath of the king: for he endured, as seeing him who is invisible. Through faith he kept the Passover, and the sprinkling of blood, lest he that destroyed the firstborn should touch them.

By faith they passed through the Red sea as by dry land: which the Egyptians assaying to do were drowned.

By faith the walls of Jericho fell down, after they were compassed about seven days. By faith the harlot Rahab perished not with them that believed not, when she had received the spies with peace" (Hebrews 11:1-31).

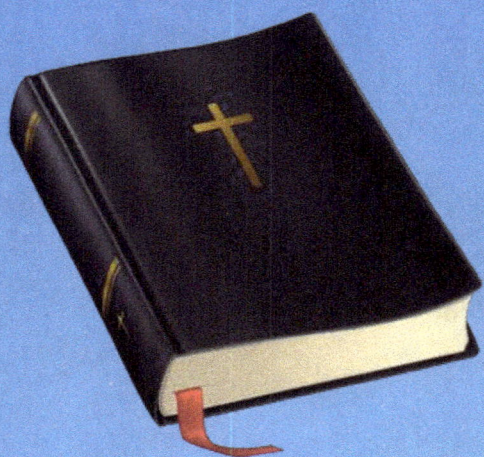

WHEN YOU ARE IN SORROW

"Let not your heart be troubled; you believe in God, believe also in Me. In My Father's house are many mansions; if it were not so, I would have told you. I go to prepare a place for you. And if I go and prepare a place for you, I will come again and receive you to Myself; that where I am, there you may be also. And where I go you know, and the way you know. Thomas said to Him, 'Lord, we do not know where You are going, and how can we know the way?' Jesus said to him, 'I am the way, the truth, and the life. No one comes to the Father except through Me. If you had known Me, you would have known My Father also; and from now on you know Him and have seen Him'."

Philip said to Him, "Lord, show us the Father, and it is sufficient for us." Jesus said to him, "Have I been with you so long, and yet you have not known Me, Philip? He who has seen Me has seen the Father; so how can you say, 'Show us the Father'? Do you not believe that I am in the Father, and the Father in Me? The words that I speak to you I do not speak on My own authority; but the Father who dwells in Me does the works. Believe Me that I am in the Father and the

Father in Me, or else believe Me for the sake of the works themselves.

"Most assuredly, I say to you, he who believes in Me, the works that I do he will do also; and greater works than these he will do, because I go to My Father. And whatever you ask in My name, that I will do, that the Father may be glorified in the Son. If you ask anything in My name, I will do it" (John 14:1-14, NKJV).

BEFORE CHURCH SERVICE

"How amiable are thy tabernacles, O Lord of host! My soul longeth, yea, even fainteth for the courts of the Lord: my heart and my flesh crieth out for the living God. Yea, the sparrow hath found an house, and the swallow a nest for herself, where she may lay her young, even thine altars, O Lord of hosts, my King, and my God. Blessed are they that dwell in thy house: they will be still praising thee. Selah. Blessed is the man whose strength is in thee; in whose heart are the ways of them. Who passing through the valley of Baca make it a well; the rain also filleth the pools. They go from strength to strength, every one of them in Zion appeareth before God. O Lord God of hosts, hear my prayer; give ears, O God of Jacob. Selah Behold, O God our shield, and look upon the face of thine anointed. For a day in thy courts is better than a thousand. I had rather be a doorkeeper in the house of my God, than to dwell in the tents of wickedness. For the Lord God is a sun and shield: the Lord will give grace and glory: no good thing will he withhold from they that walk uprightly. O Lord of host, blessed of the man that trusteth in thee" (Psalm 84).

When you have sinned

"Have mercy on me, O God, according to your steadfast love; according to your abundant mercy blot out my transgressions. Wash me thoroughly from my iniquity, and cleanse me from my sin! For I know my transgressions, and my sin is ever before me. Against you, you only, have I sinned and done what is evil in your sight, so that you may be justified in your words and blameless in your judgment. Behold, I was my mother conceive me. Behold, you delight in truth in the inward being, and you teach me wisdom in the secret heart. Purge me with hyssop, and I shall be clean; wash me, and I shall be whiter than snow. Let me hear joy and gladness; let the bones that you have broken rejoice. Hide your face from my sins, and blot out all my iniquities. Create in me a clean heart, O God, and renew a right spirit within me. Cast me not away from your presence, and take not your Holy Spirit from me. Restore to me the joy of your salvation, and uphold me with a willing spirit. Then I will teach transgressors your ways, and sinners will return to you. Deliver me from blood guiltiness, O God, O God of my salvation, and my tongue will sing aloud of your righteousness.

O Lord, open my lips, and my mouth will declare your praise" (Psalm 51, ESV).

You want to be Fruitful

"I am the true vine, and my Father is the vinedresser. Every branch in me that does not bear fruit he takes away, and every branch that does bear fruit he prunes, that it may bear more fruit. Already you are clean because of the word that I have spoken to you. Abide in me, and I in you. As the branch cannot bear fruit by itself, unless it abides in the vine, neither can you, unless you abide in me. I am the vine; you are the branches. Whoever abides in me and I in him, he it is that bears much fruit, for apart from me you can do nothing. If anyone does not abide in me he is thrown away like a branch and withers; and the branches are gathered, thrown into the fire, and burned. If you abide in me, and my words abide in you, ask whatever you wish, and it will be done for you. By this my Father is glorified, that you bear much fruit and so prove to be my disciples. As the Father has loved me, so have I loved you. Abide in my love. If you keep my commandments, you will abide in my love, just as I have kept my Father's commandments and abide in his love. These things I have spoken to you, that my joy *may be in you, and that your joy may be full"* (John 15:1-11, ESV).

WHEN YOU ARE IN DANGER

"He who dwells in the shelter of the Most High will abide in the shadow of the Almighty. I will say to the LORD, 'My refuge and my fortress, my God, in whom I trust.' For he will deliver you from the snare of the fowler and from the deadly pestilence. He will cover you with his pinions, and under his wings you will find refuge; his faithfulness is a shield and buckler. You will not fear the terror of the night, nor the arrow that flies by day, nor the pestilence that stalks in darkness, nor the destruction that wastes at noonday. A thousand may fall at your side, ten thousand at your right hand, but it will not come near you. You will only look with your eyes and see the recompense of the wicked. Because you have made the LORD your dwelling place—the Most High, who is my refuge— no evil shall be allowed to befall you, no plague come near your tent. For he will command his angel concerning you to guard you in all your ways. On their hands they will bear you up, less you strike your foot against a stone You will tread on the lion and the adder; the young lion and the serpent you will trample underfoot. 'Because he holds fast to me in love, I will

deliver him; I will protect him, because he knows my name. When he calls to me, I will answer him; I will be with him in trouble; I will rescue him and honor him. With long life I will satisfy him and show him my salvation'" (Psalm 91, ESV).

WHEN YOU HAVE THE BLUES

"I will bless the LORD at all times; his praise shall continually be in my mouth. My soul makes its boast in the LORD; let the humble hear and be glad. Oh, magnify the LORD with me, and let us exalt his name together! I sought the LORD, and he answered me and delivered me from all my fears. Those who look to him are radiant, and their faces shall never be ashamed. This poor man cried, and the LORD heard him and saved him out of all his troubles. The angel of the LORD encamps around those who fear him, and delivers them. Oh, taste and see that the LORD is good! Blessed is the man who takes refuge in him! Oh, fear the LORD, you his saints, for those who fear him have no lack! The young lions suffer want and hunger; but those who seek the LORD lack no good thing. Come, O children, listen to me; I will teach you the fear of the LORD. What man is there who desires life and loves many days, that he may see good? Keep your tongue from evil and your lips from speaking deceit. Turn away from evil and do good; seek peace and pursue it. The eyes of the LORD are toward the righteous and his *ears toward their cry. The face of the LORD is against those who do evil, to cut off the memory of them from the earth. When the righteous cry for help, the LORD hears and delivers them out of all their troubles. The LORD is near to the broken hearted and saves the crushed in spirit. Many are the afflictions of the righteous, but the LORD delivers him out of them all. He keeps all his bones; not one of them is broken. Affliction will slay the wicked, and those who hate the righteous will be condemned. The LORD redeems the life of his servants; none of those who take refuge in him will be condemned"* (Psalm 34, ESV).

WHEN YOU WORRY

"Do not lay up for yourselves treasures on earth, where moth and rust destroy and where thieves break in and steal, but lay up for yourselves treasures in heaven, where neither moth nor rust destroys and where thieves do not break in and steal. For where your treasure is, there your heart will be also. The eye is the lamp of the body. So, if your eye is healthy, your whole body will be full of light, but if your eye is bad, your whole body will be full of darkness. If then the light in you is darkness. How great is the darkness! "No one can serve two masters, for either he will hate the one and love the other, or he will be devoted to the one and despise the other. You cannot serve God and money. Therefore I tell you, do not be anxious about your life, what you will eat or what you will drink, nor about your body, what you will put on. Is not life more than food, and the body more than clothing? Look at the birds of the air: they neither sow nor reap nor gather into barns, and yet your heavenly Father feeds them. Are you not of more value than they? And which of you by being anxious can add a single hour to his span of life? And why are you anxious about clothing?

Consider the lilies of the field, how they grow: they neither toil nor spin, yet I tell you, even Solomon in all his glory was not arrayed like one of these. But if God so clothes the grass of the field, which today is alive and tomorrow is thrown into the oven, will he not much more clothe you, O you of little faith? Therefore do not be anxious, saying, 'What shall we eat?' or 'What shall we drink?' or 'What shall we wear?' For the Gentiles seek after all these things, and your heavenly Father knows that you need them all. But seek first the kingdom of God and his righteousness, and all these things will be added to you. "Therefore do not be anxious about tomorrow, for tomorrow will be anxious for itself. Sufficient for the day is its own trouble" (Matthew 6:19-34, ESV).

WHEN GOD SEEMS FAR AWAY

"O LORD, you have searched me and known me! You know when I sit down and when I rise up; you discern my thoughts from afar. You search out my path and my lying down and are acquainted with all my ways. Behold, O LORD, you know it altogether. You hem me in, behind and before, and lay your hand upon me. Such knowledge is too wonderful for me; it is high; I cannot attain it. Where shall I go from your Spirit? Or where shall I flee from your presence? If I ascend to heaven, you are there! If I make my bed in Sheol, you are there! If I take the wings of the morning and dwell in the uttermost parts of the sea, even there your hand shall lead me, and your right hand shall hold me. If I say, "Surely the darkness shall cover me, and the light about me be night," even the darkness is not dark to you; the night is bright as the day, for darkness is as light with you. For you formed my inward parts; you knitted me together in my mother's womb. I praise you, for I am fearfully and wonderfully made. Wonderful are your works; my soul knows it very well. My frame was not hidden from you, when I was being made in secret, intricately woven in the depths of the earth.

Your eyes saw my unformed substance; in your book were written, every one of them, the days that were formed for me, when as yet there was none of them. How precious to me are your thoughts, O God! How vast is the sum of them! If I would count them, they are more than the sand. I awake, and I am still with you. Oh that you would slay the wicked, O God! O men of blood, depart from me! They speak against you with malicious intent; your enemies take your name in vain. Do I not hate those who hate you, O LORD? And do I not loathe those who rise up against you? I hate them with complete hatred; I count them my enemies. Search me, O God, and know my heart! Try me and know my thoughts! And see if there be any grievous way in me, and lead me in the way everlasting!" (Psalm 139, ESV).

WHEN DOUBTS COME UPON YOU

"My doctrine is not mine, but his that sent me. If any man will do his will, he shall know of the doctrine, whether it be of God, or whether I speak of myself. He that speaketh of himself seeketh his own glory: but he that seeketh his glory that sent him, the same is true, and no unrighteousness is in him" (John 7:17).

WHEN YOU FORGET YOUR BLESSINGS

"Bless the LORD, O my soul, and all that is within me, bless his holy name! Bless the LORD, O my soul, and forget not all his benefits, who forgives all your iniquity, who heals all your diseases, who redeems your life from the pit, who crowns you with steadfast love and mercy, who satisfies you with good so that your youth is renewed like the eagle's. The LORD works righteousness and justice for all who are oppressed. He made known his ways to Moses, his acts to the people of Israel. The LORD is merciful and gracious, slow to anger and abounding in steadfast love. He will not always chide, nor will he keep his anger forever. He does not deal with us according to our sins, nor repay us according to our iniquities. For as high as the heavens are above the earth, so great is his steadfast love toward those who fear him; as far as the east is from the west, so far does he remove our transgressions from us. As a father shows compassion to his children, so the LORD shows compassion to those who fear him. For he knows our frame; he remembers that we are dust. As for man, his days are like grass; he flourishes like a flower of the field; for

the wind passes over it, and it is gone, and its place knows it no more. But the steadfast love of the LORD is from everlasting to everlasting on those who fear him, and his righteousness to children's children, to those who keep his covenant and remember to do his commandments. The LORD has established his throne in the heavens, and his kingdom rules over all. Bless the LORD, O you his angels, you mighty ones who do his word, obeying the voice of his word! Bless the LORD, all his hosts, his ministers, who do his will! Bless the LORD, all his works, in all places of his dominion" (Psalm 103, ESV).

When You Feel Down And Out

"What then shall we say to these things? If God is for us, who can be against us? He who did not spare his own Son but gave him up for us all, how will he not also with him graciously give us all things? Who shall bring any charge against God's elect? It is God who justifies. Who is to condemn? Christ Jesus is the one who died—more than that, who was raised—who is at the right hand of God, who indeed is interceding for us. Who shall separate us from the love of Christ? Shall tribulation, or distress, or persecution, or famine, or nakedness, or danger, or sword? As it is written, 'For your sake we are being killed all the day long; we are regarded as sheep to be slaughtered.' No, in all these things we are more than conquerors through him who loved us. For I am sure that neither death nor life, nor angels nor rulers, nor things present nor things to come, nor powers, nor height nor depth, nor any-thing else in all creation, will be able to separate us from the love of God in Christ Jesus our Lord" (Romans 8:31-39, ESV).

When Your Prayers grow narrow or Selfish

"God be merciful unto us, and bless us; and cause his face to shine upon us; Selah. That thy way may be known upon earth, thy saving health among all nations. Let the people praise thee, O God; let all the people praise thee. O let the nations be glad and sing for joy: for thou shalt judge the people righteously, and govern the nations upon earth. Selah. Let the people praise thee, O God; let all the people praise thee. Then shall the earth yield her increase; and God, even our own God, shall bless us. God shall bless us; and all the ends of the earth shall fear" (Psalm 67).

WHEN YOU GROW BITTER
AND CRITICAL

"This is the third time I am coming to you. Every charge must be established by the evidence of two or three witnesses. I warned those who sinned before and all the others, and I warn them now while absent, as I did when present on my second visit, that if I come again I will not spare them— since you seek proof that Christ is speaking in me. He is not weak in dealing with you, but is powerful among you. For he was crucified in weakness, but lives by the power of God. For we also are weak in him, but in dealing with you we will live with him by the power of God. Examine yourselves, to see whether you are in the faith. Test yourselves. Or do you not realize this about yourselves, that Jesus Christ is in you?—unless indeed you fail to meet the test! I hope you will find out that we have not failed the test. But we pray to God that you may not do wrong—not that we may appear to have met the test, but that you may do what is right, though we may seem to have failed. For we cannot do anything against the truth, but only for the truth. For we are glad when we are weak and you are strong. Your restoration is what we pray

for. For this reason I write these things while I am away from you, that when I come I may not have to be severe in my use of the authority that the Lord has given me for building up and not for tearing down" (2 Corinthians 13, ESV).

WHEN THE WORLD SEEMS BIGGER THAN GOD

"Lord, thou hast been our dwelling place in all generations. Before the mountains were brought forth, or ever thou hadst formed the earth and the world, even from everlasting to everlasting, thou art God. Thou turnest man to destruction; and sayest, Return, ye children of men. For a thousand years in thy sight are but as yesterday when it is past, and as a watch in the night. Thou carriest them away as with a flood; they are as a sleep: in the morning they are like grass which groweth up. In the morning it flourisheth, and groweth up; in the evening it is cut down, and withereth. For we are consumed by thine anger, and by thy wrath are we troubled. Thou hast set our iniquities before thee, our secret sins in the light of thy countenance. For all our days are passed away in thy wrath: we spend our years as a tale that is told. The days of our years are threescore years and ten; and if by reason of strength they be fourscore years, yet is their strength labour and sorrow; for it is soon cut off, and we fly away. Who knoweth the power of thine anger? even according to thy fear, so is thy wrath. So teach us to

number our days, that we may apply our hearts unto wisdom. Return, O Lord, how long? and let it repent thee concerning thy servants. O satisfy us early with thy mercy; that we may rejoice and be glad all our days. Make us glad according to the days wherein thou hast afflicted us, and the years wherein we have seen evil. Let thy work appear unto thy servants, and thy glory unto their children. And let the beauty of the Lord our God be upon us: and establish thou the work of our hands upon us; yea, the work of our hands establish thou it" (Psalm 90).

When You Want Rest And Peace

"At that time Jesus answered and said, I thank thee, O Father, Lord of heaven and earth, because thou hast hid these things from the wise and prudent, and hast revealed them unto babes. Even so, Father: for so it seemed good in thy sight. All things are delivered unto me of my Father: and no man knoweth the Son, but the Father; neither knoweth any man the Father, save the Son, and he to whomsoever the Son will reveal him. Come unto me, all ye that labour and are heavy laden, and I will give you rest. Take my yoke upon you, and learn of me; for I am meek and lowly in heart: and ye shall find rest unto your souls. For my yoke is easy, and my burden is light" (Matthew 11:25-30).

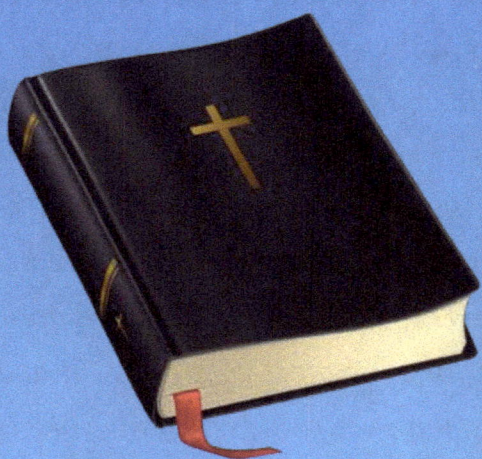

PART III

THE EFFECTIVETUDES

Effective Living is:

1. Loving God.
2. Asking God and producing fruit.
3. Knowing that God has a plan for your life.
4. Knowing that God will pull you through your problems.
5. Relying on God to do the impossible for you.
6. Including Him through acknowledgement, prayer, and thanks.
7. Consistency in faith.
8. A clean heart.
9. Strong faith.
10. Communicating is a spiritual ability.
11. Communion with God.
12. Patience in life.
13. Adhering to the appointed things God has ordained you for.
14. Obedience to God's Word.
15. Recognizing God's answers.
16. Delighting the Lord.
17. Living a righteous c lean life.

18. Fruit of the Spirit.

19. God's mercy.

20. Peace, quietness and assurance.

21. Handing your burden over to Him.

22. Deliverance from your enemy.

23. Do right, love His mercy and walk humbly.

24. Keeping your temple/body holy.

25. The Word of God dwelling inside of you.

26. The Holy Spirit in you.

27. To live in perfect peace.

28. Protection by God.

29. Discernment for false prophets.

30. Accepting Jesus as your savior.

31. Power of the Holy Spirit within you.

32. To decree a thing.

33. Knowing that God sees all things.

34. Casting all your cares to God.

35. Standing strong in you belief and faith.

36. Whatever you do "in the name of Jesus."

37. Praising from the heart.

38. Entering through the door God has opened away from sin.

39. Not blaspheming the Holy Spirit.

40. Letting go of your past.

41. Favor from God during time of trouble.

42. Experiencing the power of God.

43. Living a saved life by God.

44. Living through His spoken Words.

45. Preaching the Gospel of Jesus Christ.

46. Clinging to God's promises.

47. Living in God's shadow.

48. Believing God will make a way for you.

49. Trust in God, not man.

50. Recognizing Jesus is the Son of God.

51. An abundant life.

52. Hiding God's Word in your heart.

53. Relying on God to provide and protect.

54. Being kind and truthful.

55. God discerning the thoughts and the intentions of your heart.

56. Knowing that God cares and watches over you.

57. Overtaking blessings through God's grace.

58. Calling on Him in time of need.

59. Overcoming obstacles through God.

60. Commit your way to God.

61. Not wavering in your faith.

62. Everlasting life.

63. Committing.

64. Being the image of Christ.

65. An abundant life.

66. Choosing God.

67. The prepared life God has for you.

68. The flow of the Holy Spirit in you.

69. A life working for your good.

70. Living through the comfort that God provides.

71. Focusing on your godly assignment and on Jesus.

72. God guiding your steps in life.

73. Having an advantage over your enemy (Satan).

74. A favorable relationship with God.

75. The power of Christ in you.

76. Seeking His kingdom.

77. Not worrying.

78. Wisdom, knowledge and understanding

79. God doing the impossible for you.

80. Using your God-given power.

81. Promotion and elevation in life from God.

82. Deliverance, protection, prayer answered, support, long life, salvation and love.

83. Taking refuge in the Lord is effective living.

84. Seeing the lamp and light of Jesus in your pathway.

85. Patience in life.

86. The confidence manifested faith.

87. Petitioning God.

88. Asking God.

89. Pursuing the things of God.

90. Living a saved life through faith.

91. God's benefits.

92. An everlasting life.

93. Listening to God's voice.

References

Bible Gateway. Biblegateway.com

Bible Study - Olive Tree Bible 2016

Holy Bible Concordance - Memorial Bibles
International

Holy Bible - Thomas Nelson Publisher

Holman KJV Study Bible - Holeman Bible
Publishers

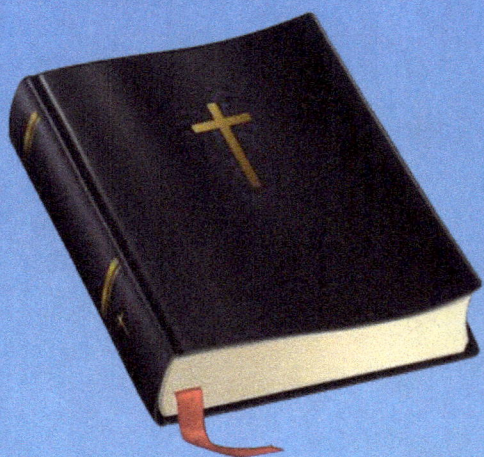

About the Author

Minister Rayford Jones Elliott is a minister of the gospel of Jesus Christ. He is a devout follower of Christ Jesus because he loves the Lord with his whole heart. As a minister, he teaches and preaches the Word with great fervency in an attempt to save the lost by bringing them into the knowledge of the truth. In his local church, where he has been a member for nineteen years. Minister Elliott serves as the president of the Men's Fellowship. He conducts weekly discussion groups, thereby demonstrating his dedication to the spiritual development of men. It is his desire to instill in them the same love and zeal for Christ Jesus he possesses.